One day at a time

Bailey Finn

BookLeaf Publishing

Presentation by *BookLeaf Publishing*

Web: www.bookleafpub.com

E-mail: info@bookleafpub.com

ISBN: 9789357615808

First edition 2022

PREFACE

The inspiration for my poetry comes from my family. I was motivated by the valuable lessons I have learnt from the incredible people in my life.

Choose Your Channel

Don't like what's on?

Stop and take a moment to be grateful for the two healthy hands you have that hold the remote.

You are lucky to have a television in front of you that the universe switches on at the start of every day.

You are always in control to choose a new channel for yourself

Planting Thoughts

The ones who can fully give,
are those truly secure in what they know

Their cup is full enough to
water the plants of others without losing
a single drop of themselves,
or ever letting go.

When your values are deeply rooted; they will
grow, and your mind will be set free

Your heart will soar far and wide,
but always be able to come back to the happy
place you have cultivated, your inner tree.

Little Cog

We are all just human beings on a big floating rock.

Just focus on putting one foot in front of the other, find what makes you happy

& be a little cog

Make Mistakes

When you're taking your first steps on
the long and rocky road of life,

Stumbles, fumbles, and rolled ankles are always
abound.

But with every trip and fall your steps become
wiser,

your footing will get better and a new stride will
be found.

Little Rock

When whirled by the unpredictable winds of
change that leave us wound in worries;
We will find ourselves swayed in many different
directions, trying to cope by being just like trees.

With every stormy season that ends, you can
never predict when another will start.
You will be faced with challenges that wither
away the wooden armor you were told to grow
thick and strong around your heart.

Weighted by the weary rains of doubts, troubles
and fears; change will seep beneath your
barricading bark, and rust even the toughest of
gears.

Shears will slash the tangled vines of lies that
you wove into a safety blanket; an unsecure
false harness of hope;

And you will be left clinging to the memories of
what was once safe and stable,
feeling like you failed, now dangling from a
crumbling cliff slope.

No matter how much you think those vines of
lies are leather reins of guidance, direction and
control;
Unfortunately, the tighter you hold onto them as
you try to steer, the further away you will
journey from your goal.

During the stampedes of change that rumble and
rattle even the toughest of trees; change is
unavoidable and discomfort will be felt in their
deepest roots, to the tips of their leaves.

The life will go on, and troubles will always
knock,
But instead of trying to be like a tree,
be patient,
be strong,

Be a Little Rock.

Poppy and Dingham

When your leaping and hopping from stone to
stone, With imagined problems and a fear of the
unknown

What isn't really here shouldn't ruin today,
made-up obstacles are never actually in your
way

So when worries about a dingham arise in your
mind,

Remember your blessings, what is real, and
leave the fiction behind

Progress is Progress

Big or small, a step in any direction is progress;
and if you don't know what way to head,
anywhere is the best way

Walking to China

We're walking to China.

Strap on your shoes and take the first step

First we walk to the beach and then maybe
hitchhike,

possibly get a bus,

up to Darwin,

Now what?

Well we get a boat across… and then I'm
thinking mopeds

Either way, at every step of the journey, don't
overthink, you're on your way

Be Here Right Now

What can I do about this right now? If there is
something I can do, do it!
If it doesn't effect now then come back and
switch into today's channel

Patience and Persistence

The hardest thing in life is to be patient

I don't know why I'm doing this, but I'm doing
it for a reason,

have patience and persistence

Perspective of Me

I am never stuck or lost,
I'm simply on my way

It's never the end road or too late for change,
The sun will rise and always bring a new day

I'm never ever alone,
I will always have my angels who surround me

I know who I am, not different or unusual,
But exactly who I am meant to be

Tomorrow

I will not worry about tomorrow's weather,
You can never know for sure when a change in
tides will rock your boat

Take it one day at a time, don't worry about the
waves you can't control, all you need to do is
float

Lessons from Dogs

1. Don't worry about what hasn't happened yet

2. Keep wagging your tail even if don't exactly know the reason you're wagging it

3. Stay curious

4. Enjoy every moment like its your last and you don't know if it will end

5. No task (stick) is ever too big

6. Keep your intentions pure

7. Love unconditionally

Look Forward

Don't think about the past, focus on where you
want to go,

Plant a seed, water each day,

and that's how you know what you truly desire
will be able to grow.

One of Those Days

Sometimes you have one of those days where
you are surrounded by people but still feel pretty
lonely,

All you want to do is go home to the comfort of
your family, but sometimes even your family
can't give you that confront because it turns out
they have had ones of those days too,

I those cases, all you can do is be there for each
other and go to bed knowing that you'll wake up
to a better tomorrow.

Negative Into Positive

Never Backwards, not doing bad is always good,
and if you know that you've done good, you can
sleep happy.

If it stops the negative, then it's positive.

When you're thinking about todays choices, big
or small, not doing bad is always good.

And if you've done good, then you can sleep
happy and proud knowing that you've
accomplished everything you could.

Just Breathe

Deep breath in…

Center yourself and watch what you thought
were troubles become blessings, and your big
obstacle lead you to win…

And out …

relax from the constant changes that come
because even the most still of mountains stand
strong, but we're formed on a planet that will
always continue to spin…

Lemonade

Slow is smooth and smooth is fast

Don't rush yourself and your goals if you want
them to last

If you want to be rest easy at night then work
hard and you're bed will be made

It won't be easy or exactly what you expect, but
when life gives you lemons, make lemonade

Don't Think, Just Do!

Come back to today, stop thinking and start
using your brain,

When you create your own obstacles, you inflict
your own pain.

Get out of your way by doing more of 'just do',

Don't overthink, follow your heart and simply
trust you

Serenity

Grant the serenity to accept the things I can not change,

Courage to change the things I can,

And the wisdom to know the difference.

Just Keep Swimming Finn

When things don't go to plan,

and for something different you were wishing...

take on whatever life has put in front of you,

trust the process,

and remember that, hey...

at least we're fishing!

www.ingramcontent.com/pod-product-compliance
Lightning Source LLC
LaVergne TN
LVHW050302200726
843509LV00015B/3116